KU-213-119

The Flower Seeds

EDUCATIONAL AND READING CONSULTANTS

Diana Bentley and Dee Reid, Senior Lecturers in Language and Reading,
Oxford Brookes University

Published by Evans Brothers Limited
2A Portman Mansions
Chiltern Street
London, W1U 6NR

First published in this edition 2005

First published in 1994
Reprinted 1997, 1998, 2007

Printed in Hong Kong by New Era Printing Co., Ltd

ISBN 0 237 52934 3

ACKNOWLEDGEMENTS

Planning and production by Discovery Books
Edited by Kate Johnson
Designed by Ian Winton
Typesetting by The Image Bureau

For permission to reproduce copyright material, the author and publishers
gratefully acknowledge the following:
Heather Angel: cover (top left) and page 6; Chris Fairclough: page 9; Image Bank: cover
(bottom) and pages 23 and 27; Alex Ramsay: pages 13, 14, 18; Topham: page 29.

The Flower Seeds

Rosie Hankin

Illustrated by Nick Ward

Dad is going to plant seeds in the garden.

4

These seeds will grow into the biggest plants in the garden.

Wait and see.

7

Digging lets more air into
the soil and this helps the
seeds grow.

Now the seeds can be
planted.

10

The seeds will grow roots in the soil.

The seeds have sprouted.
Now they are called
seedlings.

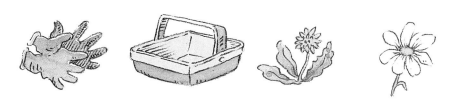

The seedlings are growing quickly.

15

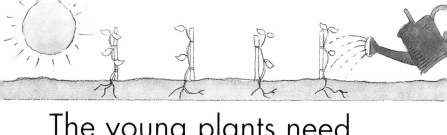

The young plants need
support.

*I'm tying the
stems to these stakes.*

18

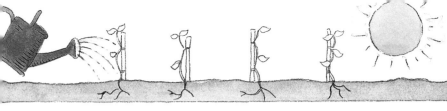

Plants need food from the soil. They also need sunlight and water.

19

Soon you will see what kind of plants you have grown.

The flower heads are as big
as dinner plates.

The sunflowers are only twenty weeks old but they are very tall.

They are taller than Dad.

24

25

Look at the bees on the flowers.

26

The bees are collecting a
sweet liquid called nectar.

The sunflowers have lost all their petals. The flower heads have dried.

Look, they're full of seeds.

We'll plant the seeds
next year.

29

Look at this picture of the
stages of a sunflower. Can
you point to the seedling,
roots, stem, leaves, bud,
flower head, seeds
and petals?

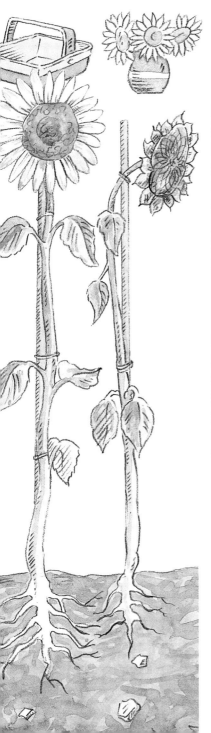

Index